To JACK

LOVE FROM AUNTIE MARGUERITE
XXX

A Treasury For
Little Ones

Introduction

From my experience as a mother and a childcare worker, I know how satisfying it is to discover a new book for your child that can be used time and time again. The volume that you are now holding will, I feel, be one such book to enjoy together – popular with you as well as your children!

There is an enormously wide range of activities and ideas included in the book – suitable for "activity times" when you can't get out and about for whatever reason, and for "snuggle-down-together times".

Play is vital for all babies and toddlers, and the educational dimension of play has long been recognized. The beautifully detailed illustrations in this book offer many ways to learn through play.

The clear, bright "Alphabet animal" pages give a lovely opportunity to try out first letter sounds, making recognition fun. The "Make and play" pages help to develop fine motor control and creative skills.

Taken as a whole, this nursery collection provides ample practice for all your child's early learning skills.

Have fun!

Jo Thomas, NNEB

A Treasury For
Little Ones

Hours of fun for babies and toddlers
– stories and rhymes, puzzles to solve,
and things to make and do

NICOLA BAXTER AND MARIE BIRKINSHAW
ILLUSTRATED BY FRANK ENDERSBY

ARMADILLO

This edition is published by Armadillo, an imprint of Anness Publishing Ltd,
108 Great Russell Street, London WC1B 3NA; info@anness.com

www.annesspublishing.com

If you like the images in this book and would like to investigate using them for publishing,
promotions or advertising, please visit our website www.practicalpictures.com
for more information.

Publisher: Joanna Lorenz
Produced by: Nicola Baxter
Editorial consultant: Ronne Randall
Designer: Amanda Hawkes
Production designer: Amy Barton
Production controller: Wendy Lawson

PUBLISHER'S NOTE
Although the advice and information in this book are believed to be accurate and true
at the time of going to press, neither the authors nor the publisher can accept any legal
responsibility or liability for any errors or omissions that may have been made nor for
any inaccuracies nor for any loss, harm or injury that comes about from following
instructions or advice in this book.

Manufacturer: Anness Publishing Ltd, 108 Great Russell Street,
London WC1B 3NA, England
For Product Tracking go to: www.annesspublishing.com/tracking
Batch: 4690-22895-1127

Contents

Tickling rhymes!

Round and round the garden

Round and round the garden
Like a teddy bear,
One step,
Two steps,
Tickle you under there!

Pat-a-cake

Pat-a-cake! Pat-a-cake! Baker's man,
Bake me a cake as fast as you can.
Pat it and prick it and mark it with B,
And put it in the oven for Baby and me!

This little piggy

This little piggy went to market.

This little piggy stayed at home.

This little piggy had roast beef.

This little piggy had none.

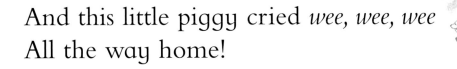

And this little piggy cried *wee, wee, wee*
All the way home!

Action rhymes

The wheels on the bus

The wheels on the bus go round and round,
Round and round, round and round,
The wheels on the bus go round and round,
All day long.

The wipers on the bus go swish, swish, swish,
Swish, swish, swish, swish, swish, swish,
The wipers on the bus go swish, swish, swish,
All day long.

The bell on the bus goes ding, ding, ding,
Ding, ding, ding, ding, ding, ding,
The bell on the bus goes ding, ding, ding,
All day long.

The children on the bus bounce up and down,
Up and down, up and down,
The children on the bus bounce up and down,
All day long.

Can you make up some more verses
about what happens on the bus?

The grand old Duke of York

Oh, the grand old Duke of York
He had ten thousand men;
He marched them up to the top
    of the hill,
And he marched them down again.

And when they were up, they were up,
And when they were down, they were down,
And when they were only halfway up,
They were neither up nor down.

Peter and Paul

Two little birds sat on
    a wall,
One named Peter,
One named Paul.
Fly away, Peter!
Fly away, Paul!
Come back, Peter!
Come back, Paul!

Counting Rhymes

One, two, three, four, five

One, two, three, four, five,
Once I caught a fish alive,
Six, seven, eight, nine, ten,
Then I let it go again.

Why did you let it go?
Because it bit my finger so!
Which finger did it bite?
This little finger on the right!

Baa, baa, black sheep

Baa, baa, black sheep,
Have you any wool?
Yes, sir, yes, sir,
Three bags full.
One for my master,
And one for my dame,
And one for the little boy
Who lives down the lane.

One, two, buckle my shoe

One, two, buckle my shoe;
Three, four, knock at the door;
Five, six, pick up sticks;
Seven, eight, lay them straight;
Nine, ten, my fat hen;
Eleven, twelve, dig and delve;
Thirteen, fourteen, maids a-courting;
Fifteen, sixteen, maids in the kitchen;
Seventeen, eighteen, maids in waiting;
Nineteen, twenty, my plate's empty.

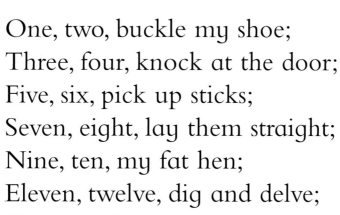

Bedtime rhymes

Star song

Star light, star bright,
First star I see tonight,
I wish I may, I wish I might,
Have the wish I wish tonight.

Jack, be nimble

Jack, be nimble,
Jack, be quick,
Jack, jump over the candlestick!

How many miles to Babylon?

How many miles to Babylon?
Three score miles and ten.
Can I get there by candlelight?
Yes, and back again.
If your heels are nimble and light,
You may get there by candlelight.

Hush-a-bye, baby

Hush-a-bye, baby, on the treetop,
When the wind blows, the cradle will rock;
When the bough breaks, the cradle will fall,
Down will come baby, cradle and all.

Diddle, diddle, dumpling

Diddle, diddle, dumpling, my son John,
Went to bed with his trousers on!
One shoe off and one shoe on,
Diddle, diddle, dumpling, my son John.

The Ugly Duckling

Mother Duck

ducklings

ugly duckling

lake

reeds

watched as five fluffy hatched from the eggs in her nest. Then waited for the last egg to hatch. At last, the egg cracked. Out came a very ! The other laughed at him.

showed the how to swim on the cool, blue . But the just hid in the , because the other laughed at him.

led her little ones into the . But the hid behind the straw, because the other laughed at him.

The  was so sad that he ran away. All through winter he stayed away from the big  . When spring came, the  saw some white birds flying in the  .

barn

sky

swan

One swan called to the  . "How beautiful you are!" he said. "Come and join us!"

The  looked at himself in the water. He wasn't an  any more! He was a beautiful  !

And the  never laughed at him again.

Chicken Licken

Chicken Licken

king

Henny Penny

Goosey Loosey

Turkey Lurkey

One day  was coming out of her house when OUCH! something fell on her head. "Oh, no! The sky is falling down!" said  . "I must go and tell the !"

On the way,  met  and  . "The sky is falling down, and I'm going to tell the ," said  . "Please come too!"

So  ,  and  went on their way until they met  . "The sky is falling down, and I'm going to tell the ," said  "Please come too!"

So  , , and went on their way. But someone was listening. It was ! "I'll pretend to be the !" he said. And he put a royal sign upon his .

Foxy Loxy

door

acorn

Soon  , , and arrived. They knocked at the and saw… ! Quickly, they slammed the and ran all the way back to 's house. On the ground was an .

"I think this is what hit you," said . "We don't need to tell the after all!"

Three Little Pigs

pigs

straw

wolf

sticks

Once there were three little .
The first little pig built a house of
. But when the big bad
came along, he huffed and he puffed
and he blew the house down with a
CRASH!

The second little pig built a house of
. But when the big bad
came along, he huffed and he puffed
and he blew the house down with a
CRUNCH!

The third little pig built a house

of  . But when the big bad

 came along, he could not

blow the  down!

He huffed and puffed and puffed and

huffed. But still the big bad

could not blow the  down.

bricks

house

The  was angry and climbed

down the  . But the third little

pig was ready. He put a

under the  . Then SPLASH!

That was the end of the

big bad  !

chimney

cooking pot

The Three Bears

cottage

porridge

Goldilocks

bowl

chair

It was breakfast time at the three bears' . But the  was too hot, so the bears went for a walk. Now, was also in the forest. She smelt the  and went inside the .

 tried the big  and the medium  . But the  in the little tiny  was just right. So she ate it all up!

 sat in the big and the medium . But the little tiny was just right … until it broke into pieces!

 went upstairs. She tried the big  and the medium . But the little tiny  was just right, and she fell fast asleep.

bed

The three bears came back to the . They saw the . They saw the . They saw the . They saw .

bowls

Suddenly the little girl woke up and saw the three bears. Quickly she ran out of the and was never seen again.

chairs

beds

Three Billy Goats

grass

river

bridge

greedy troll

the first
billy goat

The Three Billy Goats Gruff wanted to eat the  on the other side of the . But a guarded the only .

 went to cross the .
Trip, trap, trip, trap!
UP jumped the . "I'll eat you for my breakfast!" he roared.
"Don't eat me!' said _____.
"Eat _____. He's much fatter than I am." So the _____ let him pass.

Then _____ went to cross the _____.
Trip, trap, trip, trap!
UP jumped the _____. "I'll eat you for my breakfast!" he roared.

"Don't eat me!' said .

"Eat . He's much fatter than

I am." So the let him pass.

the second
billy goat

Then went to cross the .

Trip, trap, trip, trap!

UP jumped the . "I'll eat

you for my breakfast!" he roared.

"Oh, no, you won't!" bellowed .

He tossed the over the

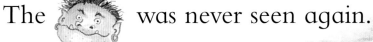 and SPLASH! into the .

The was never seen again.

the third
billy goat

The Big Pancake

old lady

flour

pan

Big Pancake

door

One day an  decided to make some pancakes. She mixed some , some milk and an egg together, and poured the mixture into a hot .

At once she heard someone shouting, "I'm the , nice and hot! You won't catch me, no, certainly not!" The  leapt out of the  and on to the floor. It rolled right out of the .

"Stop!" cried the .

The  rolled and rolled. It rolled past a  and a  . But it didn't stop.

The  rolled past a  and a  . But it didn't stop.

dog

cat

horse

Then the  came to the place where  stood.  put out his snout and made the  trip. Then he tossed it and gave it a flip. "Mm, a  nice and not hot!"

cow

With one big gulp,  ate the lot!

Big Pig

Another you!

You will need:

mirror

roll of old wallpaper

pencil

red, yellow, blue and
white poster paints

wool the same shade
as your hair

white glue

paintbrush

baking tray

Ask a grown-up to help you make
this very familiar person!

1 Roll the wallpaper out flat on
the floor.

2 Lie down on the wallpaper and ask
your helper to draw around you.

3 Look in the mirror. What shade are your eyes, hair, skin and clothes?

4 Now decorate the wallpaper person to look just like you. Stick on wool to make hair.

5 Pour paint into the baking tray and make foot and hand prints on a separate piece of paper. When they are dry, cut them out and stick them on your person.

You can mix all the paints you need from four pots of paint.

red + yellow = orange

blue + yellow = green

red + blue = purple

red + blue + yellow = brown

red + white = pink
Mix brown, pink, white and yellow for skin tones.

Funny clown face

You will need:

large plate

scissors

wool or string

thin cardboard

elastic (not too thin)

white glue

pencil

paint and brush

Ask a grown-up to help you make this magnificent mask!

1 Draw around the plate on to some cardboard.

2 Draw some hair, a hat and a tie on to the circle.

3 Ask your grown-up helper to cut around the face and make holes for your eyes.

4 Stick on wool or string for hair.

5 Stick on a large red cardboard nose.

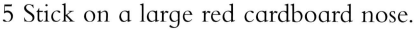

6 Make a red banana shape for a mouth, with string lips in the middle.

7 Decorate the rest of the face, hat and tie with paints or pieces of cardboard. The clown faces on these pages will give you some ideas.

8 Ask your helper to make a hole either side of the mask and knot the elastic through. Check it is not too tight.

9 Have fun being a clown!

Can you do some funny clown tricks?

Do a wobbly clown's walk.

Make silly clown noises.

Try to juggle some beanbags.

Chocolate crispies

You will need:

mixing bowl

spoon

10 cupcake liners

100g (3oz) cooking chocolate

50g (2 cups) crispy rice cereal

10ml (2 tsp) golden or light corn syrup

5ml (1 tsp) hot water

5ml (1 tsp) margarine

25g (2 tbsp) chopped dried apricots

Ask a grown-up to help you make these yummy treats!

Wash your hands and put on an apron before you start.

1 Ask your grown-up helper to melt the chocolate in a microwave or over hot water and then mix in the syrup, hot water and margarine.

2 Put the crispy cereal in a mixing bowl and pour in the warm chocolate mixture. Stir quickly with a spoon until all the crispy cereal is covered with chocolate. Then add the chopped apricots.

You could try these ingredients instead of the apricots:

raisins

cherries

mini marshmallows

3 Fill the cupcake liners with the mixture and leave the crispies to cool.

4 Have fun sharing your crispies!

chocolate chips

other confectionery

A royal crown

You will need:

thin cardboard

pencil and ruler

crayons and paints

scissors

white glue

adhesive tape
or staples

decorations

Ask a grown-up to help you make
this lovely crown!

Follow the patterns below with your
finger. Which one will you choose?

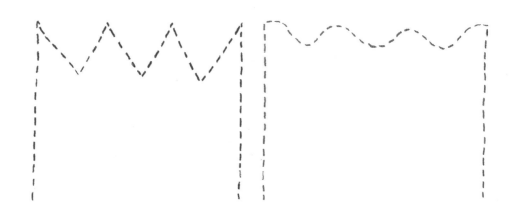

1 Ask your grown-up helper to cut a piece of cardboard at least 20cm (8in) deep and long enough to go around your head.

2 Show your helper what kind of pattern you would like along the top. Help to draw it so the grown-up can cut it out.

3 Decorate your crown. You could use paints or crayons, then stick on any decorations you like.

4 When the glue is dry, help to bend the crown round and fix it with tape or staples.

5 Enjoy being a King, Queen, Princess or Prince!

Wear your crown to sing some royal rhymes. Do you know these ones?

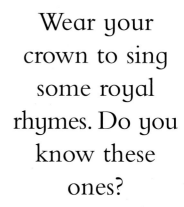

The Queen of Hearts

Old King Cole

Pussy Cat, Pussy Cat

Picnic mix-up

Giraffe is last to arrive for a picnic in the park. Use your finger to help him find the way and collect up all the food that his friends have dropped.

Giraffe has lots of friends!
What are they all doing?

Rainbow route

Help the rainbow-makers find their way over the mountains to their rainbow machine. Make sure you pass all the paints they need to make a rainbow.

What else can you see in the picture?

In the woods

Use your finger to follow the path through the woods. Can you name the woodland creatures that you meet along the way? What else can you see?

Bedtime bear

It is Bubbly's bedtime, but all her night-time things are in the wrong place!

Follow the path through Bubbly's house to find everything she needs for a good night's sleep.

What do you like to have at bedtime?

Jump and jiggle

1 Can you?

Can you wriggle 10 fingers and then jiggle 10 toes?

2

Can you do 9 jumps and then wiggle 1 nose?

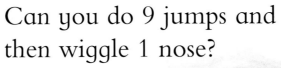

3

4 Can you clap 8 times and then pat 2 knees?

5

Can you do 7 skips and then
SNEEZE SNEEZE SNEEZE?

Can you do 6 bends and
then 4 hops?

Now count to 5 and
then shout, "STOP!"

6

7

8

9

10

Finger wiggles

Clench your fist to make a beehive.

Peep into your pretend beehive.

Gently unfold one finger at a time, pretending to make the bees fly away!

The busy beehive

Here is the busy beehive.
Where are the busy bees?

Hidden away where nobody sees.
Soon they come creeping out of the hive.

One…
  Two…
    Three…
      Four…
        Five…

BUZZ! BUZZ! BUZZ! BUZZ! BUZZ!

Five little soldiers

Five little soldiers standing in a row.
Three are standing straight.
And two stand so.

Stand the fingers and thumb of one hand up in a line like soldiers.

Along comes the Captain,
And what do you think?

Up

Bend two fingers as if they are resting.

March the thumb of your other hand across to the "soldier" fingers.

All five "soldier" fingers stand to attention.

jump the soldiers, quick as a wink!

Noisy farmyard

calf

foal

piglet

lamb

duckling

chick

Neigh!

Baa!

Can you match the mothers and babies at the side of the picture?

cow

horse

pig

sheep

duck

hen

On the beach

Can you find all the little pictures
in the big picture?

sandcastle

sun

iced lolly

bucket and spade

waves

beach ball

How many different shades
can you see on the beach?

crab

beach chair

seaweed

beach umbrella

starfish

sailboat

Shopping

oranges

cheese

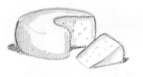

tomatoes

milk

juice

bread

Can you find all the little pictures in the big picture?

What do you like to
buy when you go shopping?

shopping basket

shopping cart

cash register

money

shopping bag

receipt

On the move

Can you find all the little pictures in the big picture?

car

van

dumper truck

tanker

bus

digger

What sounds do
these vehicles make?

train

plane

canal boat

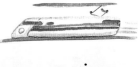

motorcycle

bicycle

hot-air balloon

Aa Aa Aa Aa Aa

Andy Ant is an angry
ant on an acorn.

artist

acrobat

armchair

What else begins with **a**?

aircraft

astronaut

anchor

ambulance

apple

actor

Bb Bb Bb Bb Bb

ball

bed

bell

bubbles

bath

banana

book

Billy Bear is batting a ball.

What else begins with **b**?

bee

bag

buttons

butterfly

bus

bicycle

bottle

building bricks

boat

balloon

Cc Cc Cc Cc Cc

cow

clown

Carrie Camel has come
to a coconut.

castle

camera

crab

What else begins with **c**?

car

candle

cabbage

C

clock

cake

carrot

calendar

Dd Dd Dd Dd Dd

dragon

desert

dog

door

Dora Duck is dipping
deep down.

digger

doctor

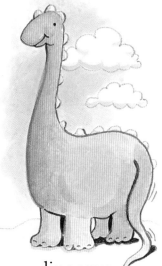

dinosaur

dentist

What else begins with **d**?

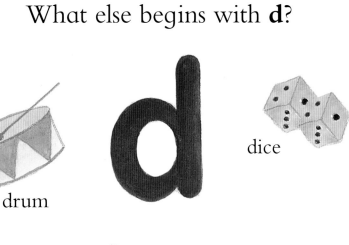

d

dice

drum

dancer

drawing

Ee Ee Ee Ee Ee

eagle

escalator

ears

eggs

envelope

Elsie Elephant is eating an enormous egg.

What else begins with **e**?

elephant

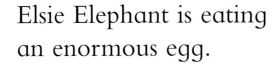

entrance

exit

explorer

Ff Ff Ff Ff Ff Ff

Fiona is a friendly fish.

frog

fireworks

fountain

flowers

farm

fire

flamingo

What else begins with **f**?

footprint

fish

f

flag

feather

flour

fork

Gg Gg Gg Gg Gg

Gary Goat has grown
some green grapes.

gate

glue

grass

grain

grasshopper

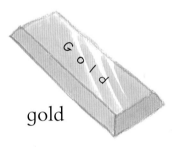

gold

What else begins with **g**?

guitar

garden

g

grapes

glider

glass

Hh Hh Hh Hh

helicopter

hand

house

Hugo Hippo is still hugely hungry.

What else begins with **h**?

hat

hammer

hospital

helmet

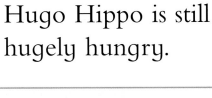

hill   hair

h

happy

heart

horse

Ii Ii Ii Jj Jj Jj Jj

iron

igloo

invitation

ink

ice cream

iceberg

Iggy Iguana is itching and
Julia Jellyfish is jiggling.

Scratch!
Scratch!

What else begins with **i** or **j**?

Jeep

juice

juggler

jigsaw
puzzle

jewels

Kk Kk Kk Kk

kissing

key

kicking

Kelly Koala keeps
kittens in the kitchen.

What else begins with **k**?

king

kite

kitten

kangaroo

k

keyhole

kiwi

Ll Ll Ll Ll Ll Ll

Lucy Lion has lost
her lizard.

lamb

ladybird
or ladybug

leaf

lightning

lawnmower

label

What else begins with **l**?

luggage

lemon

ladder

lunchbox

leopard

Mm Mm Mm

moon

monkey

magnet

Mary Mouse is making a mess.

What else begins with **m**?

mirror

mountain

motorcycle

mermaid

m

money

magician

milk

Nn Nn Nn Nn

Norman and the Newts
are noisy but nice.

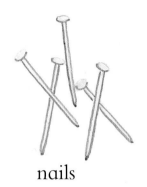

nails

night

necklace

nurse

newspaper

What else begins with **n**?

nest

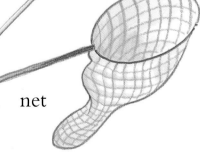

needle

net

Oo Oo Oo Oo

ostrich

oranges

oars

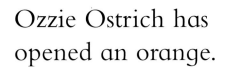

Ozzie Ostrich has
opened an orange.

owl

office

oboe

What else begins with **o**?

octopus

oven

oil

Pp Pp Pp Pp Pp

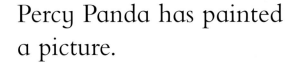

Percy Panda has painted
a picture.

pencil

penguin

pear

pumpkin

polar
bear

pan

pixie

What else begins with **p**?

pen

paper

p

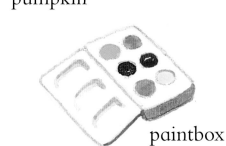
paintbox

present

pond

parrot

puzzle

Qq Qq Qq Qq

Queenie Quail is quick and quiet.

queen

quilt

queue

Ssshhh!

Quiet!

What else begins with **qu**?

Quack!

qu

quarter

questions

Rr Rr Rr Rr Rr

Rosie Rabbit races
down the river.

robot

rain

ruler

ribbon

rainbow

river

ring

raccoon

What else begins with **r**?

rocket

rocking horse

raspberry

roof

rhinoceros

Ss Ss Ss Ss Ss Ss

star

starfish

ship

stairs

Sally Snake is sipping her spicy soup.

What else begins with **s**?

snail

seagull

spaghetti

swan

submarine

stamp

shell

spaceship

scissors

spider

Tt Tt Tt Tt Tt

table

trunk

telephone

turtle

Tilly Turtle has taken a taxi.

Taxi

What else begins with **t**?

trumpet

train

toothpaste

toothbrush

tree

tiger

tent

t

towel

Uu Uu Uu Uu

upside down

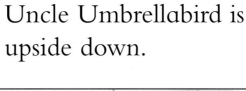

Uncle Umbrellabird is upside down.

umbrella

undressing

unicorn

What else begins with **u**?

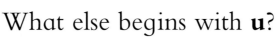

untied

untidy

Oh no!

under

Vv Vv Vv Vv

Valerie Vole makes vegetables vanish.

vulture

vacuum cleaner

video cassette

volcano

vase

What else begins with **v**?

violin

V

vegetables

van

Ww Ww Ww

Wanda Whale washes the windows with waves.

windmill

wheel

wolf

well

waterfall

watch

What else begins with **w**?

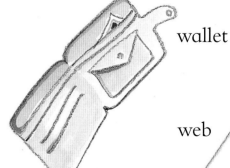
wallet

web

wheelbarrow

whistle

Xx Xx Xx Xx

mixing

Foxy Loxy plays the xylophone.

What else has an **x** sound?

ox

6

six

fox

x–ray

taxi

boxes

exit

Yy Yy   Zz Zz

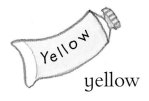
yellow

Yakkety Yak yawns as Zippy Zebra zooms around the zoo.

zebra

yo-yo

0

zero

yolk

What else begins with **y** or **z**?

y **z**

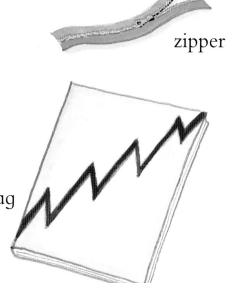
zipper

yawn

yogurt

zigzag

Alphabet fun

a b c
d e f
g h i
j k l
m n o
p q r
s t u
v w x
y z

Look back through the book to find these pictures. What letter sound begins their names? Can you point to that letter?

Have fun singing the alphabet to the tune of *The Grand old Duke of York*, or another well-known nursery rhyme.

Number fun hunt

Go on a page-hunt to find:

Rhymes index

Can you remember these?